HAL•LEONARD
UKULELE
PLAY-ALONG

Standards

CONTENTS

Ukulele by Chris Kringel

ISBN 978-1-4584-1874-6

HAL•LEONARD®
CORPORATION

7777 W. Bluemound Rd. P.O. Box 13819 Milwaukee, WI 53213

Visit Hal Leonard Online at
www.halleonard.com

Ain't Misbehavin'

Words by Andy Razaf
Music by Thomas "Fats" Waller and Harry Brooks

TRACK 1

First note

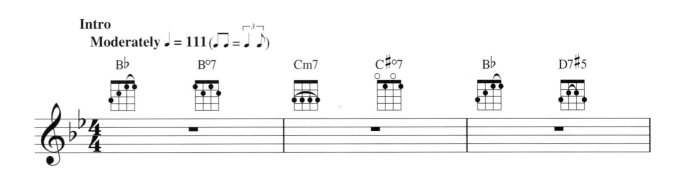

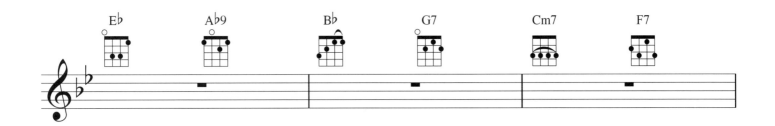

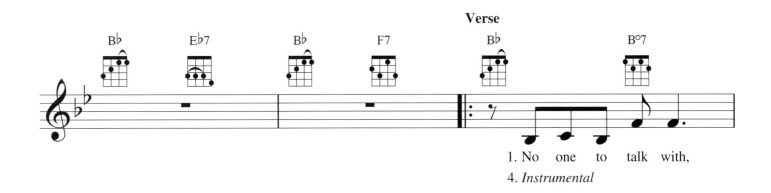

1. No one to talk with,
4. *Instrumental*

all by my-self. No one to walk with, but I'm hap-py on the shelf. ___

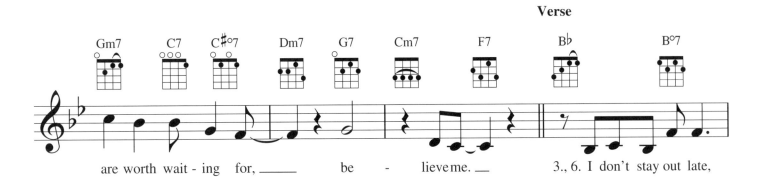

are worth wait - ing for, _____ be - lieve me. _____ 3., 6. I don't stay out late,

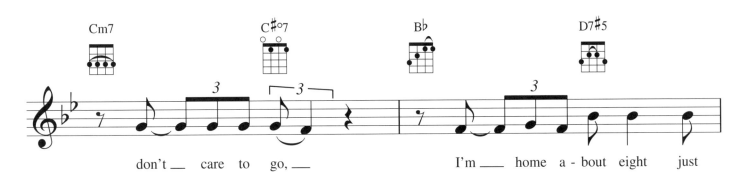

don't _ care to go, _ I'm _ home a - bout eight just

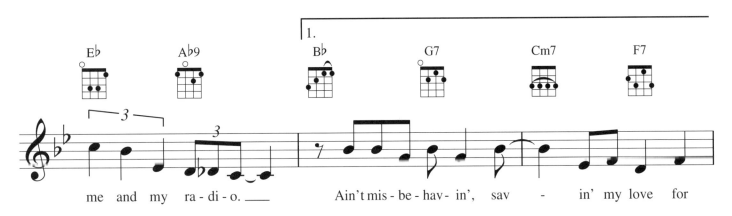

me and my ra - di - o. _____ Ain't mis - be - hav - in', sav - in' my love for

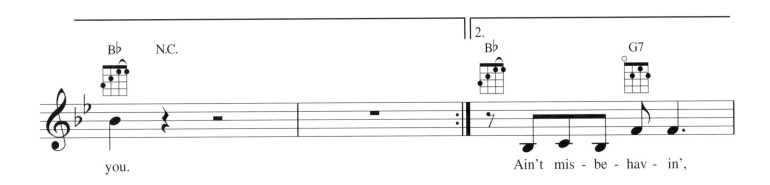

you. Ain't mis - be - hav - in',

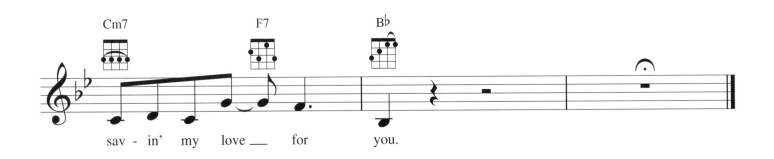

sav - in' my love _ for you.

TRACK 7

Georgia on My Mind

Words by Stuart Gorrell
Music by Hoagy Carmichael

First note

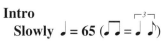

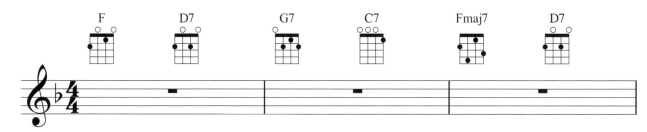

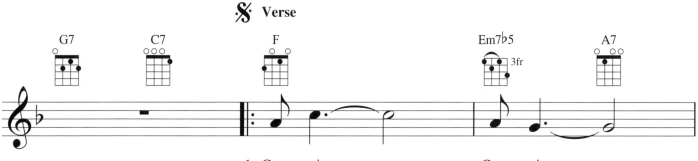

1. Geor - gia, _____   Geor - gia, _____
2. Geor - gia, _____   Geor - gia, _____
4. *Instrumental*

the   whole   day   through.   Just   an   old   sweet   song __   keeps
a   song   of   you   comes as   sweet   and   clear __   as

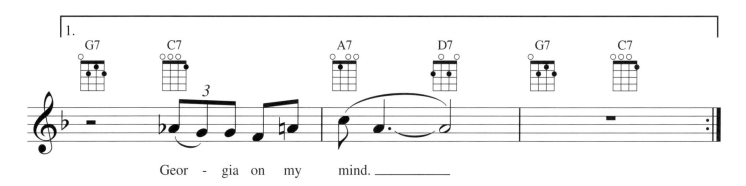

Geor - gia on my mind. _____

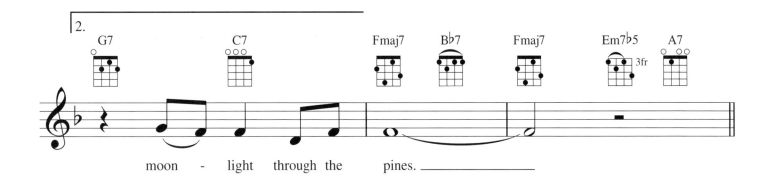

moon - light through the pines. _____

Bridge

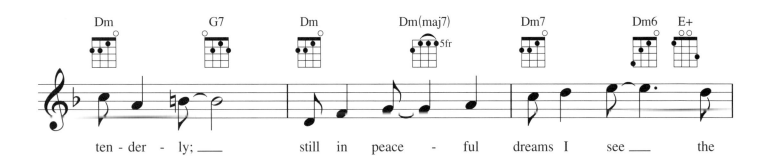

Oth - er arms ___ reach out to me; ___ oth - er eyes ___ smile

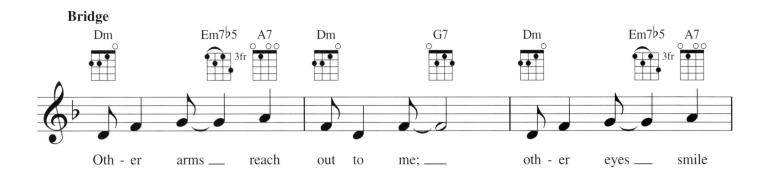

ten - der - ly; ___ still in peace - ful dreams I see ___ the

Verse

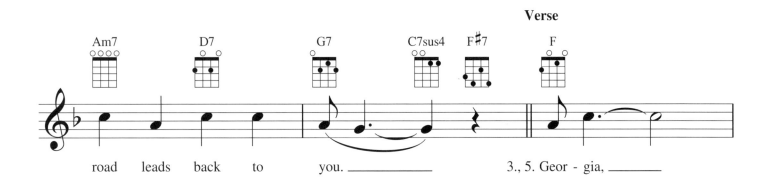

road leads back to you. _____ 3., 5. Geor - gia, ___

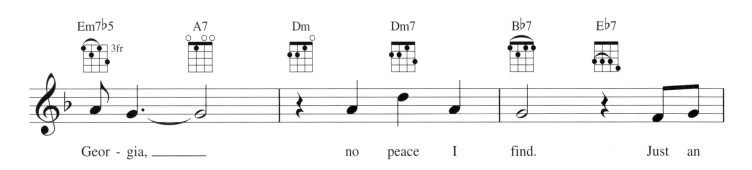

Geor - gia, ___ no peace I find. Just an

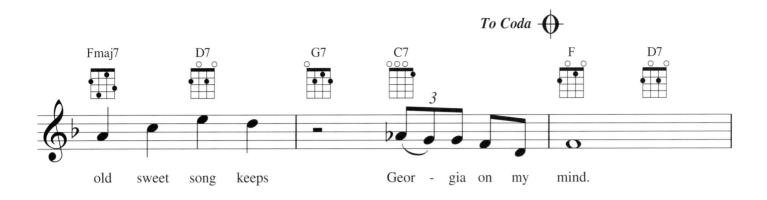

old sweet song keeps Geor - gia on my mind.

D.S. al Coda
(take 2nd ending)

Coda

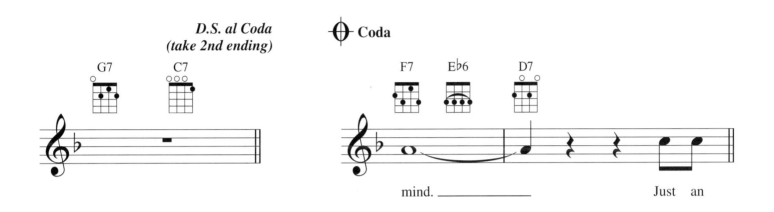

mind. _____ Just an

Outro

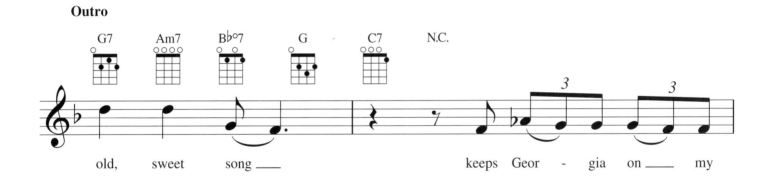

old, sweet song ___ keeps Geor - gia on ___ my

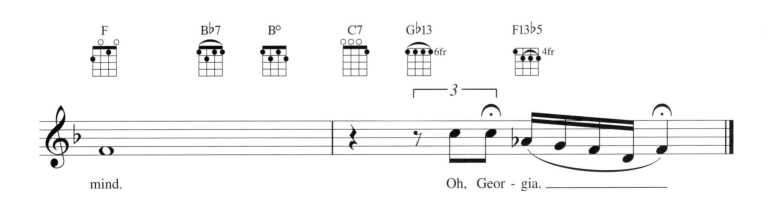

mind. Oh, Geor - gia. _____

All of Me

Words and Music by Seymour Simons and Gerald Marks

First note

Verse
Moderately fast ♩ = 140

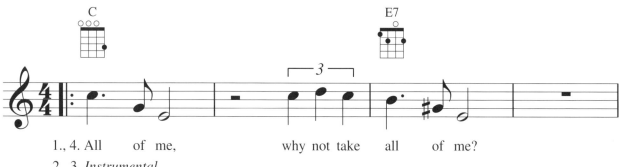

1., 4. All of me, why not take all of me?
2., 3. *Instrumental*

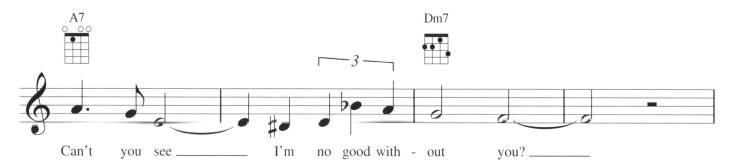

Can't you see _____ I'm no good with - out you? _____

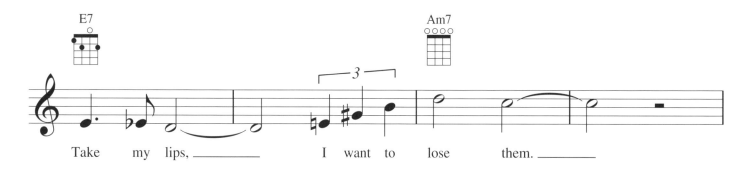

Take my lips, _____ I want to lose them. _____

Take my arms, _____ I'll nev - er use them.

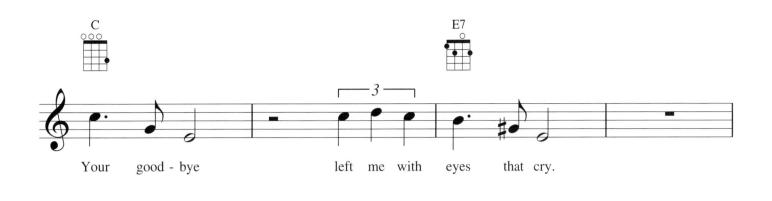

Your good-bye left me with eyes that cry.

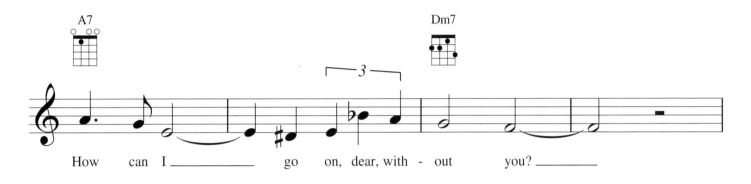

How can I _____ go on, dear, with-out you? _____

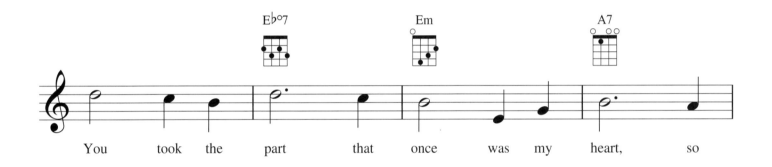

You took the part that once was my heart, so

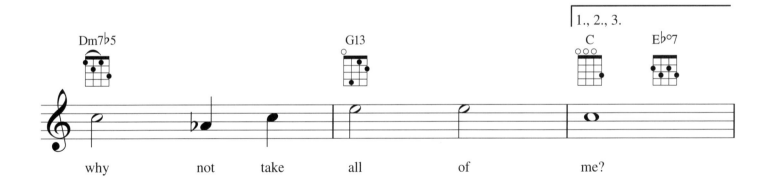

why not take all of me?

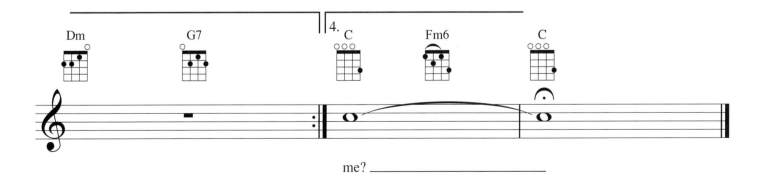

me? _____

Beyond the Sea

Lyrics by Jack Lawrence
Music by Charles Trenet and Albert Lasry
Original French Lyric to "La Mer" by Charles Trenet

Some - where _____ be - yond the sea, some - where wait - ing for me, _____ my lov - er stands on gold - en sands _____ and watch - es the ships that go sail - ing. Some- where _____ be - yond the sea, she's there watch - ing for me. _____ If I could fly like birds on high, _____ then straight to her

Mister Sandman

Lyric and Music by Pat Ballard

First note

Intro
Moderately ♩ = 107
N.C.

Bom, bom, bom, bom, bom, bom, bom, bom,

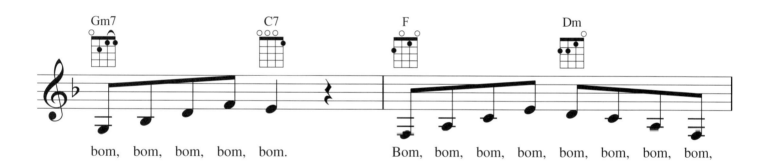

bom, bom, bom, bom, bom.

Bom, bom, bom, bom, bom, bom, bom, bom,

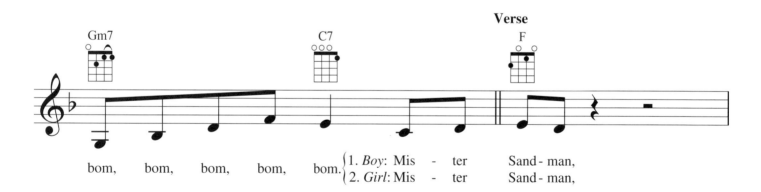

bom, bom, bom, bom, bom.

{ 1. *Boy*: Mis - ter Sand - man,
{ 2. *Girl*: Mis - ter Sand - man,

bring me a dream, __ make her com - plex-ion like peach - es and cream. __
bring me a dream, __ make him the cut - est that I've ev - er seen. __

Moon River

from the Paramount Picture BREAKFAST AT TIFFANY'S

Words by Johnny Mercer
Music by Henry Mancini

TRACK 11

First note

Intro
Moderately slow ♩ = 95

Verse

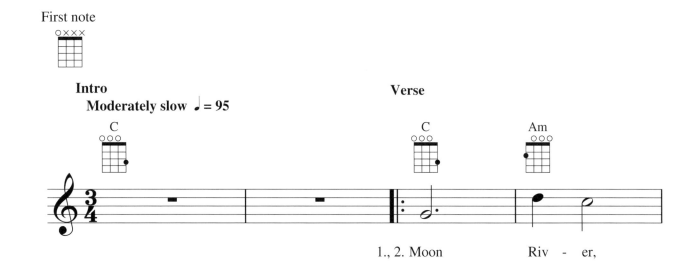

1., 2. Moon Riv - er,

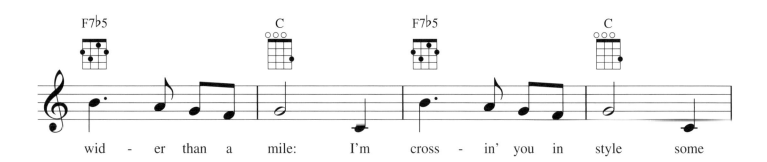

wid - er than a mile: I'm cross - in' you in style some

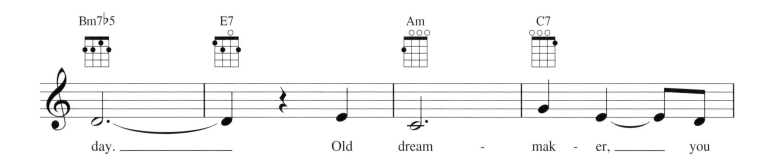

day. _____ Old dream - mak - er, _____ you

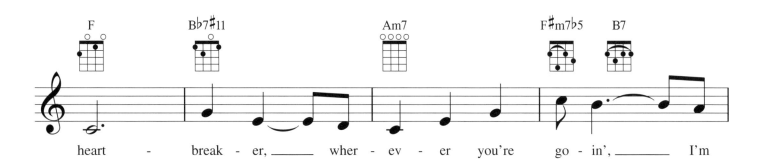

heart - break - er, _____ wher - ev - er you're go - in', _____ I'm

That's Amoré
(That's Love)
from the Paramount Picture THE CADDY

Words by Jack Brooks
Music by Harry Warren

First note

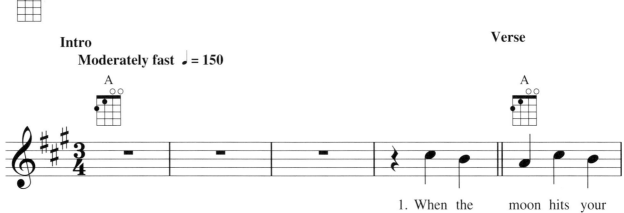

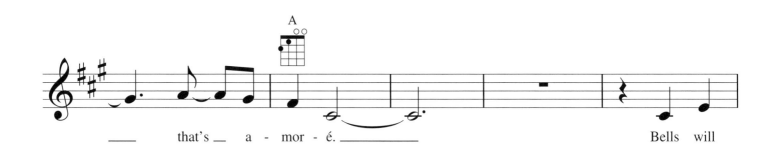

ring, ting-a-ling-a - ling, ting-a-ling-a - ling, and you'll sing, "Vi - ta Bel - la." ____

____ Hearts will play, tip-py, tip-py tay, tip-py, tip-py tay, like a

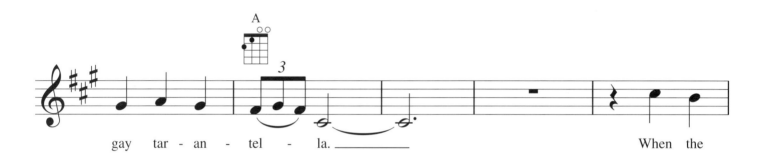

gay tar-an-a-tel - la. _____ When the

stars make you drool just like pas-ta fa - zool, __ that's _ a - mor - é. ____

____ When you dance down the street with a

cloud at your feet you're _ in love. _____

When you walk ___ in a dream, but you know you're not dream - ing, Si -

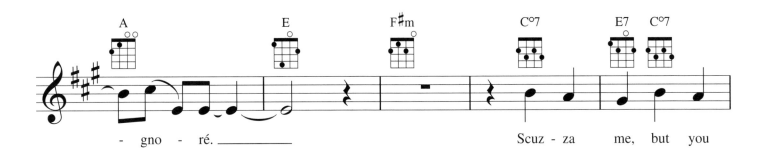

- gno - ré. _____ Scuz - za me, but you

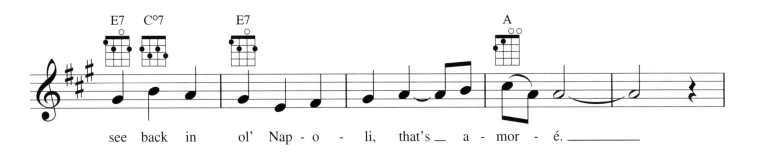

see back in ol' Nap - o - li, that's ___ a - mor - é. _____

Verse

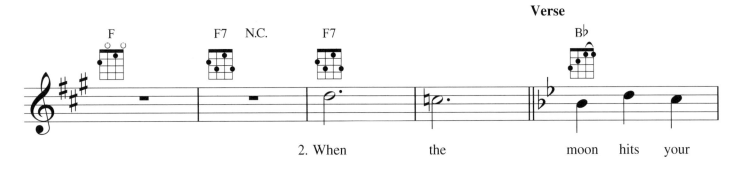

2. When the moon hits your

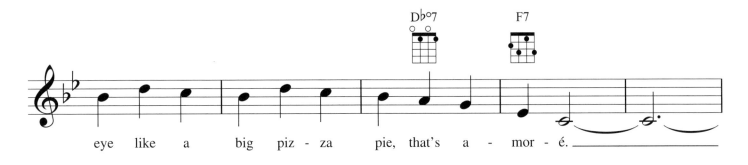

eye like a big piz - za pie, that's a - mor - é. _____

___ When the world seems to shine like you've had too much

wine, that's a - mor - é. _____ Bells will

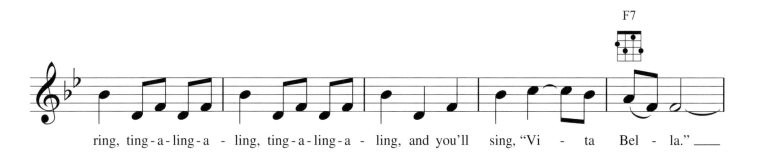

ring, ting-a-ling-a- ling, ting-a-ling-a- ling, and you'll sing, "Vi - ta Bel - la." ___

_____ Hearts will play, tip - py, tip - py - tay, tip - py, tip - py -

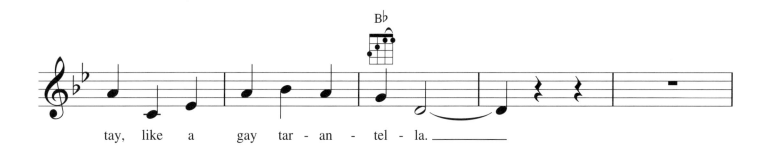

tay, like a gay tar - an - tel - la. _____

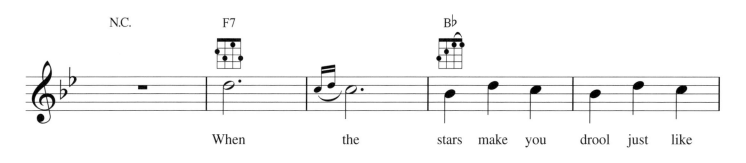

When the stars make you drool just like

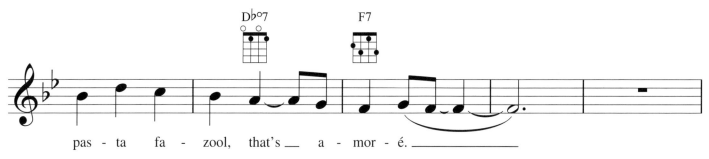

pas - ta fa - zool, that's __ a - mor - é. _____

When you dance down the street with a cloud at your feet, you're in

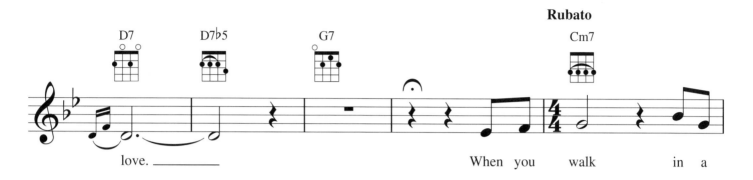

Rubato

| D7 | D7♭5 | G7 | | Cm7 |

love. _____ When you walk in a

A tempo

| E♭ | E♭m | B♭ |

dream, but you know you're not dream - ing, Si - gno - ré. _____

| Gm | D♭°7 | F7 D♭°7 | F7 D♭°7 | F7 |

Scu - za me, but you see back in ol' Nap - o -

| B♭ | G♭ | F7 |

li, that's __ a - mor - é. _____ That's __ a -

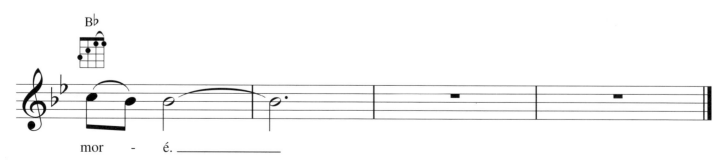

| B♭ |

mor - é. _____

TRACK 15

Unchained Melody

from the Motion Picture UNCHAINED

Lyric by Hy Zaret
Music by Alex North

First note

Chorus
Slowly ♩. = 67

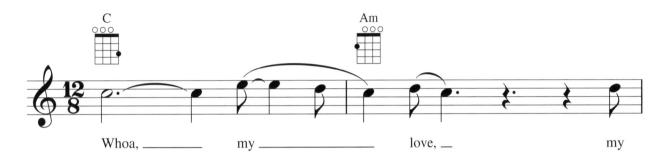

Whoa, _____ my _____ love, _____ my

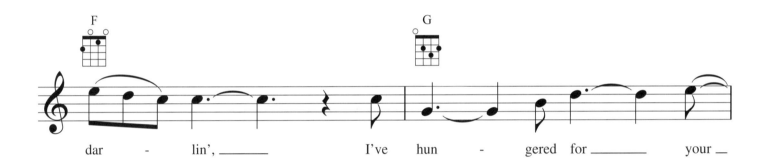

dar - lin', _____ I've hun - gered for _____ your _____

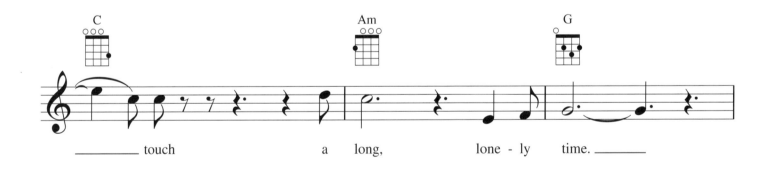

_____ touch a long, lone - ly time. _____

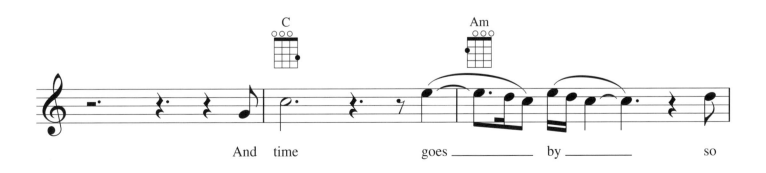

And time goes _____ by _____ so

slow - ly _____ and time can do so _____

_____ much. Are _____ you _____ still

mine? _____ I _____ need _ your love.

I _____ need your love. _____ God

To Coda ⊕

speed your love _____ to _____ me. ____

HAL·LEONARD UKULELE PLAY-ALONG

Now you can play your favorite songs on your uke with great-sounding backing tracks to help you sound like a bona fide pro!

1. POP HITS
American Pie • Copacabana (At the Copa) • Crocodile Rock • Kokomo • Lean on Me • Stand by Me • Twist and Shout • What the World Needs Now Is Love.
00701451 Book/CD Pack......................$14.99

2. UKE CLASSICS
Ain't She Sweet • Five Foot Two, Eyes of Blue (Has Anybody Seen My Girl?) • It's Only a Paper Moon • Living in the Sunlight, Loving in the Moonlight • Pennies from Heaven • Tonight You Belong to Me • Ukulele Lady • When I'm Cleaning Windows.
00701452 Book/CD Pack......................$12.99

3. HAWAIIAN FAVORITES
Aloha Oe • Blue Hawaii • HarborLights • The Hawaiian Wedding Song (Ke Kali Nei Au) • Mele Kalikimaka • Sleepy Lagoon • Sweet Someone • Tiny Bubbles.
00701453 Book/CD Pack......................$12.99

4. CHILDREN'S SONGS
Do-Re-Mi • The Hokey Pokey • It's a Small World • My Favorite Things • Puff the Magic Dragon • Sesame Street Theme • Splish Splash • This Land Is Your Land.
00701454 Book/CD Pack......................$12.99

5. CHRISTMAS SONGS
Do You Hear What I Hear • Feliz Navidad • Frosty the Snow Man • Here Comes Santa Claus (Right down Santa Claus Lane) • Jingle-Bell Rock • Nuttin' for Christmas • Rudolph the Red-Nosed Reindeer • Santa Claus Is Comin' to Town.
00701696 Book/CD Pack......................$12.99

6. LENNON & McCARTNEY
And I Love Her • Day Tripper • Here, There and Everywhere • Hey Jude • Let It Be • Norwegian Wood (This Bird Has Flown) • Nowhere Man • Yesterday.
00701723 Book/CD Pack......................$12.99

7. DISNEY FAVORITES
Alice in Wonderland • The Bare Necessities • Candle on the Water • Chim Chim Cher-ee • A Dream Is a Wish Your Heart Makes • Mickey Mouse March • Supercalifragilisticexpialidocious • Under the Sea.
00701724 Book/CD Pack......................$12.99

8. CHART HITS
All the Right Moves • Bubbly • Hey, Soul Sister • I'm Yours • Toes • Use Somebody • Viva la Vida • You're Beautiful.
00701745 Book/CD Pack......................$14.99

9. THE SOUND OF MUSIC
Climb Ev'ry Mountain • Do-Re-Mi • Edelweiss • Maria • My Favorite Things • Sixteen Going on Seventeen • Something Good • The Sound of Music.
00701784 Book/CD Pack......................$12.99

10. MOTOWN
Baby Love • Easy • How Sweet It Is (To Be Loved by You) • I Heard It Through the Grapevine • I Want You Back • My Cherie Amour • My Girl • You Can't Hurry Love.
00701964 Book/CD Pack......................$12.99

11. CHRISTMAS STRUMMING
Away in a Manger • Deck the Hall • The First Noel • Hark! the Herald Angels Sing • Jingle Bells • Joy to the World • O Come, All Ye Faithful (Adeste Fideles) • We Three Kings of Orient Are.
00702458 Book/CD Pack......................$12.99

12. BLUEGRASS FAVORITES
Angel Band • Dooley • Fox on the Run • I Am a Man of Constant Sorrow • I'll Fly Away • Keep on the Sunny Side • Sitting on Top of the World • With Body and Soul.
00702584 Book/CD Pack......................$12.99

13. UKULELE SONGS
Daughter • Dream a Little Dream of Me • Elderly Woman Behind the Counter in a Small Town • Last Kiss • More ThanYou Know • Sleepless Nights • Tonight You Belong to Me • Yellow Ledbetter.
00702599 Book/CD Pack......................$12.99

14. JOHNNY CASH
Cry, Cry, Cry • Daddy Sang Bass • Folsom Prison Blues • Hey, Porter • I Walk the Line • Jackson • (Ghost) Riders in the Sky (A Cowboy Legend) • Ring of Fire.
00702615 Book/CD Pack......................$14.99

15. COUNTRY CLASSICS
Achy Breaky Heart (Don't Tell My Heart) • Chattahoochee • Crazy • King of the Road • Rocky Top • Tennessee Waltz • You Are My Sunshine • Your Cheatin' Heart.
00702834 Book/CD Pack......................$12.99

16. STANDARDS
Ain't Misbehavin' • All of Me • Beyond the Sea • Georgia on My Mind • Mister Sandman • Moon River • That's Amoré (That's Love) • Unchained Melody.
00702835 Book/CD Pack......................$12.99

17. POP STANDARDS
Every Breath You Take • Fields of Gold • I Just Called to Say I Love You • Kansas City • Killing Me Softly with His Song • Sunny • Tears in Heaven • What a Wonderful World.
00702836 Book/CD Pack......................$12.99

23. TAYLOR SWIFT
Crazier • Fearless • Love Story • Mean • Our Song • Teardrops on My Guitar • White Horse • You Belong with Me.
00704106 Book/CD Pack......................$14.99

24. WINTER WONDERLAND
All I Want for Christmas Is My Two Front Teeth • Blue Christmas • The Christmas Song (Chestnuts Roasting on an Open Fire) • Have Yourself a Merry Little Christmas • Let It Snow! Let It Snow! Let It Snow! • Little Saint Nick • Sleigh Ride • Winter Wonderland.
00101871 Book/CD Pack......................$12.99

HAL·LEONARD® CORPORATION

7777 W. BLUEMOUND RD. P.O. BOX 13819 MILWAUKEE, WI 53213

www.halleonard.com

Prices, contents, and availability subject to change without notice.

0912